HORSE FARM

CLYDESDALE HORSES

ANNE ACCARDI

NorwoodHouse Press

Cataloging-in-Publication Data

Names: Accardi, Anne.
Title: Clydesdale horses / Anne Accardi.
Description: Buffalo, NY : Norwood House Press, 2027. | Series: Horse farm | Includes glossary and index.
Identifiers: ISBN 9781978580862 (pbk.) | ISBN 9781978580879 (library bound) | ISBN 9781978580886 (ebook)
Subjects: LCSH: Clydesdale horse--Juvenile literature.
Classification: LCC SF293.C65 A33 2027 | DDC 636.15--dc23

Published in 2027 by
Norwood House Press
2544 Clinton Street
Buffalo, NY 14224

Designer: Rhea Magaro
Editor: Kim Thompson

Photo credits: Cover, p. 1 LaurieSH/Shutterstock.com; p. 5 SA Tourist/Shutterstock.com; p. 6 Serenity Images23/Shutterstock.com; p. 7 SKOVAX/Shutterstock.com; p. 8 OlesyaNickolaeva/Shutterstock.com; p. 9 E.Druz/Shutterstock.com; p. 10 Balooelf/Shutterstock.com; p. 11 VDB Photos/Shutterstock.com; p. 13 Conny Sjostrom/Shutterstock.com; p. 14 Stephen Barnes/Shutterstock.com; p. 16 Wikipedia; p. 17 GIMP 2.10; p. 18 Joy Brown/Shutterstock.com; p. 19 Kenneth William Caleno/Shutterstock.com; p. 21 Olga_i/Shutterstock.com;

Printed in the United States of America

CPSIA compliance information: Batch #CSNHP27: For further information contact Norwood House Press at 1-800-237-9932.

TABLE OF CONTENTS

Meet the Clydesdale Horse

The Clydesdale is one of the largest horse **breeds**. Clydesdales are giants, but they are **docile** and friendly.

Clydesdales were first bred in Scotland hundreds of years ago.

They are draft horses. That means they can pull heavy loads.

What Do Clydesdales Look Like?

Like all horses, Clydesdales have a **mane**, a tail, and four **hooves**.

Their hair is mostly brown, black, and red. They have long, feathery, white hair on their legs.

Clydesdales are huge. They stand as tall as an adult man. They weigh thousands of pounds.

Their hooves can be
as big as frying pans!

How Do Clydesdales Help People?

Clydesdales are strong and powerful. They are also calm and steady. They make good workers!

On the farm, Clydesdales are used for **hauling**.

They help move tools and supplies.

Clydesdales pull wagons and **carriages**.

You may see them in parades. When they **trot**, they lift their feet high.

What Do Clydesdales Need?

Big Clydesdales need lots of food and water.

They eat grass, **hay**, and grains.

A Clydesdale's long leg hair needs daily **grooming**.

Their hooves should be trimmed often. They need extra large **horseshoes**!

Glossary

breeds (breeds): types or kinds of an animal

carriages (KAR-ij-is): vehicles that are pulled by horses and that people can ride in

docile (DAH-suhl): calm and easy to manage or train

grooming (GROO-ming): combing, brushing, and cleaning

hauling (HAWL-ing): pulling or dragging

hay (hay): long grass that is cut, dried, and used as food for farm animals

hooves (hoovz): hard parts that cover the feet of horses, pigs, and other animals

horseshoes (HORS-shooz): pieces of U-shaped metal that are nailed to the bottom of a horse's hooves to provide protection

mane (mayn): long, thick hair that grows on a horse's head and neck

trot (traht): to move faster than walking but slower than running

Thinking Questions

1. What country do Clydesdales come from?
2. What is a draft horse?
3. Why are Clydesdales good workers?
4. How big are Clydesdales?
5. Why are Clydesdales used in parades?

Index

About the Author

Anne Accardi is a librarian who loves reading books and learning new things! She lives in Kansas City, Missouri. When she's not writing, Anne enjoys listening to music, exploring nature around the city, and spending time with her family.